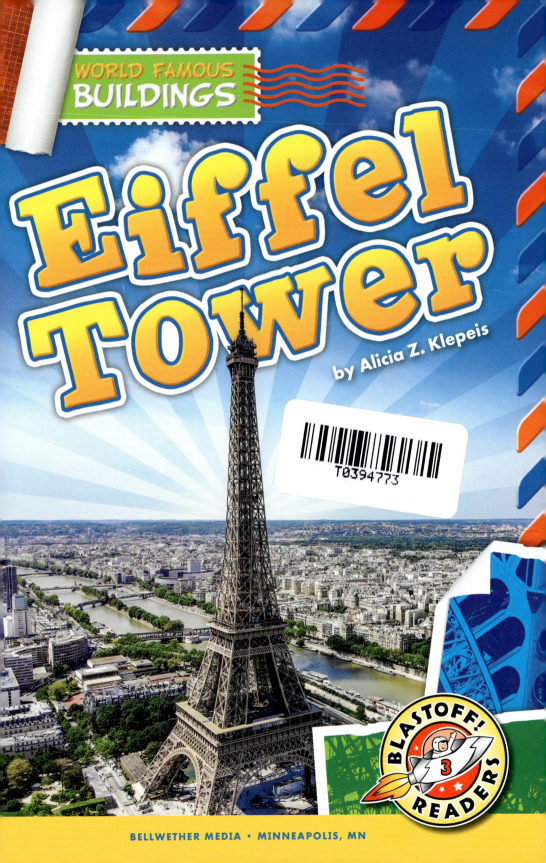

WORLD FAMOUS BUILDINGS

Eiffel Tower

by Alicia Z. Klepeis

BELLWETHER MEDIA • MINNEAPOLIS, MN

Blastoff! Readers are carefully developed by literacy experts to build reading stamina and move students toward fluency by combining standards-based content with developmentally appropriate text.

 Level 1 provides the most support through repetition of high-frequency words, light text, predictable sentence patterns, and strong visual support.

 Level 2 offers early readers a bit more challenge through varied sentences, increased text load, and text-supportive special features.

 Level 3 advances early-fluent readers toward fluency through increased text load, less reliance on photos, advancing concepts, longer sentences, and more complex special features.

★ **Blastoff! Universe**

Reading Level

Grade K

Grades 1–3

Grade 4

This edition first published in 2026 by Bellwether Media, Inc.

No part of this publication may be reproduced in whole or in part without written permission of the publisher. For information regarding permission, write to Bellwether Media, Inc., Attention: Permissions Department, 3500 American Blvd W, Suite 150, Bloomington, MN 55431.

Library of Congress Cataloging-in-Publication Data

LC record for Eiffel Tower available at: https://lccn.loc.gov/2025018613

Text copyright © 2026 by Bellwether Media, Inc. BLASTOFF! READERS and associated logos are trademarks and/or registered trademarks of Bellwether Media, Inc. Bellwether Media is a division of FlutterBee Education Group.

Editor: Megan Borgert-Spaniol   Series Designer: Chase Demmin

Printed in the United States of America, North Mankato, MN.

Table of Contents

What Is the Eiffel Tower? 4
History of the Eiffel Tower 8
Parts of the Eiffel Tower 14
The Eiffel Tower Today 18
Glossary 22
To Learn More 23
Index 24

What Is the Eiffel Tower?

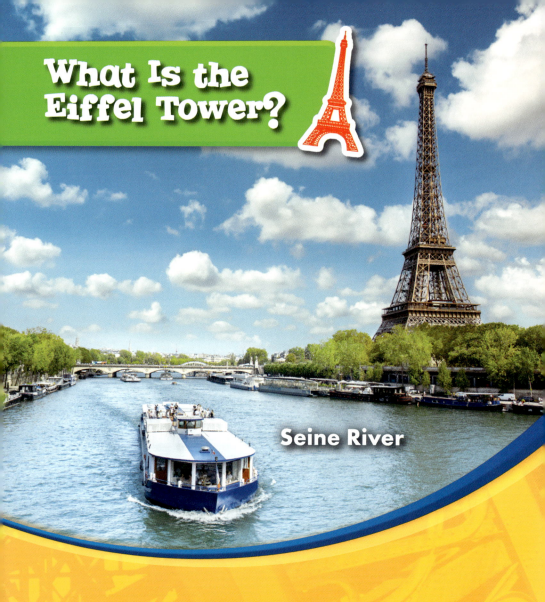

Seine River

The Eiffel Tower is a famous **monument**. It stands along the Seine River in Paris, France.

It was the world's tallest tower for over 40 years!

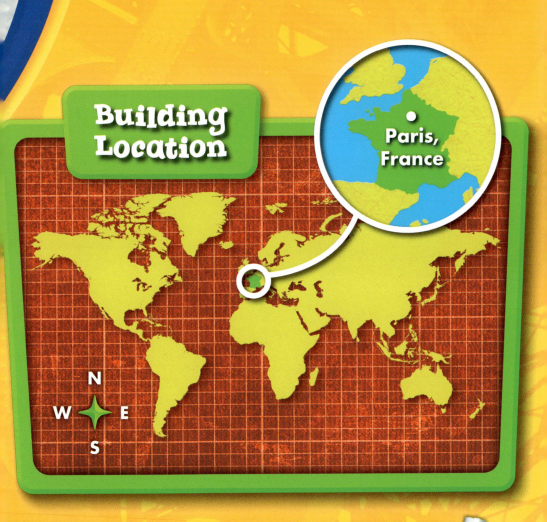

Many **tourists** visit the Eiffel Tower. They go up the tower for amazing views.

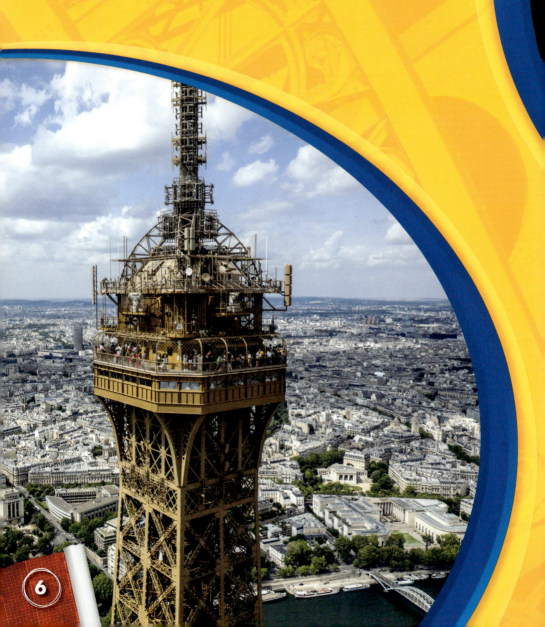

Lights make the tower sparkle at night.

History of the Eiffel Tower

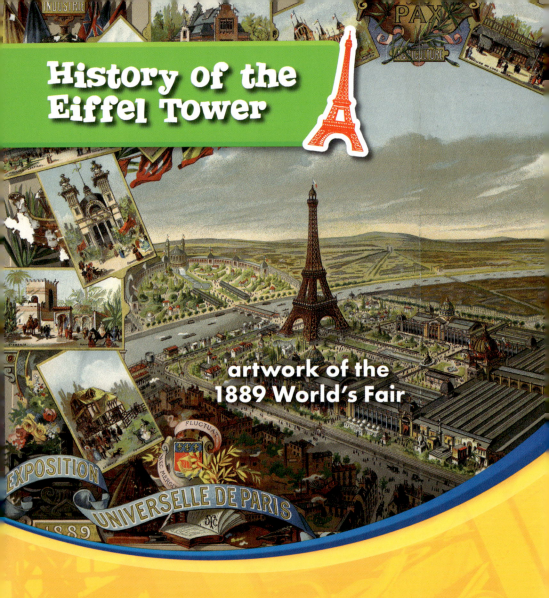

artwork of the 1889 World's Fair

In 1886, French leaders were planning the 1889 World's Fair. They held a contest to **design** a monument for it.

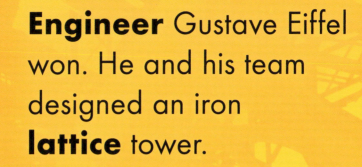

Engineer Gustave Eiffel won. He and his team designed an iron **lattice** tower.

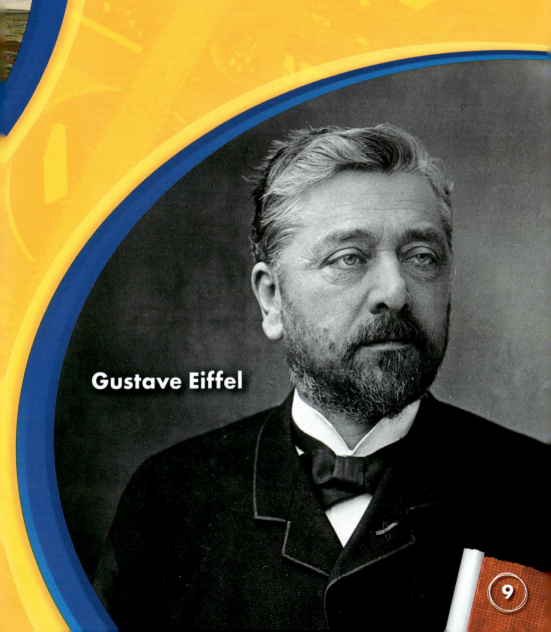

Gustave Eiffel

The tower's **concrete** base was built in 1887. The tower's legs were added next. They help the tower stand against the wind.

Girders were added to connect the tower's legs. **Architect** Stephen Sauvestre added arches between the tower's legs.

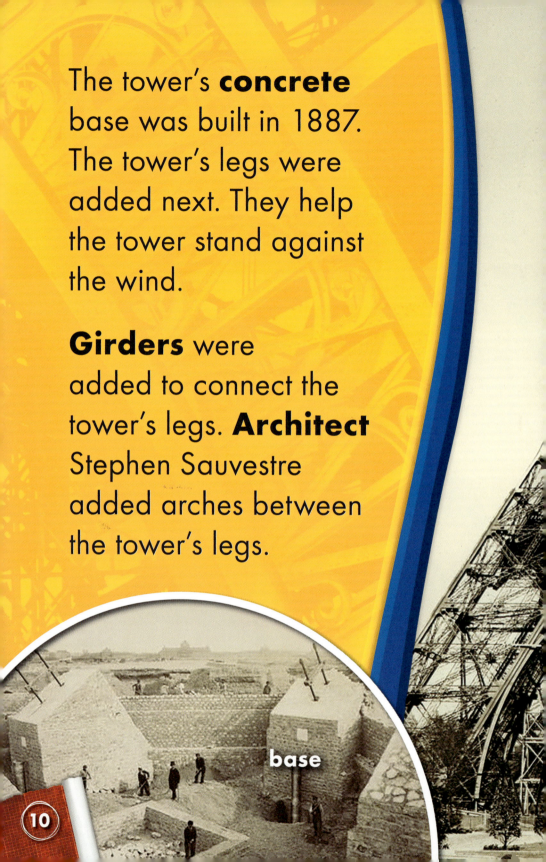

base

The Eiffel Tower was finished in 1889. It was built from around 18,000 iron pieces.

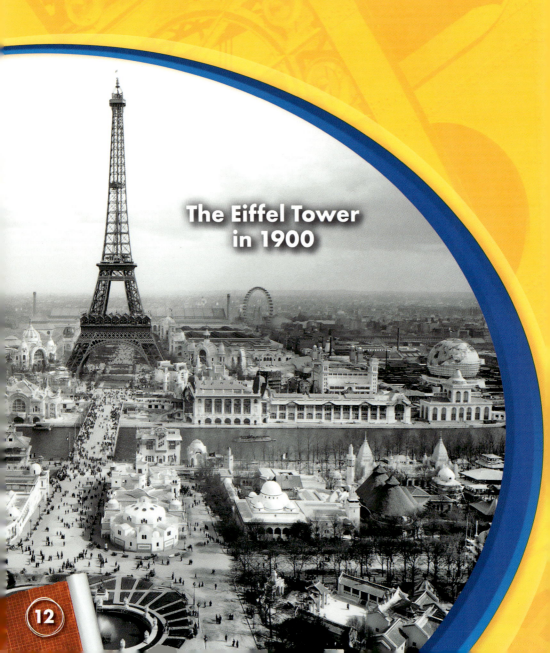

The Eiffel Tower in 1900

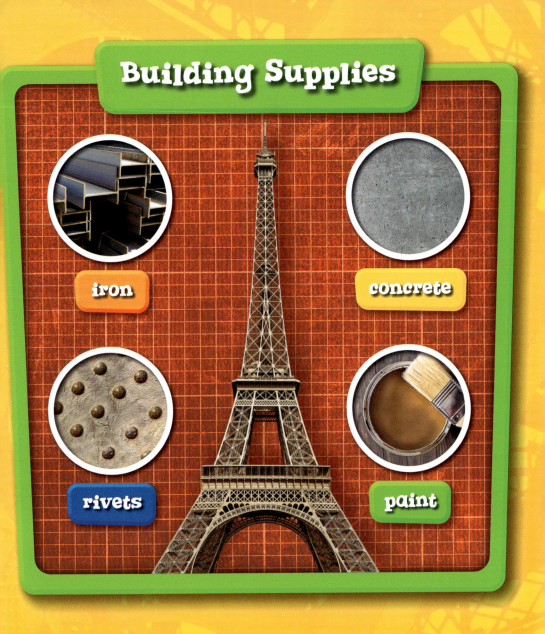

Builders used around 2.5 million **rivets** to connect the pieces!

Parts of the Eiffel Tower

French leaders planned to remove the Eiffel Tower after 20 years. Gustave Eiffel saved the tower by giving it more uses. He added a science lab and a **telegraph** station.

Restaurants and shops were later added to draw tourists.

Le Jules Verne

Height off the Ground: 410 feet (125 meters)

Famous For: restaurant with huge windows that show amazing views of Paris

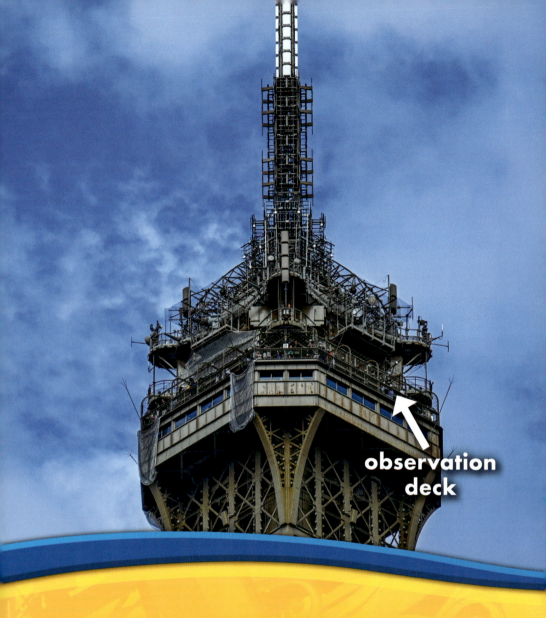

observation deck

The Eiffel Tower was originally 1,024 feet (312 meters) tall. Radio and TV **antennas** added 59 feet (18 meters) to the tower.

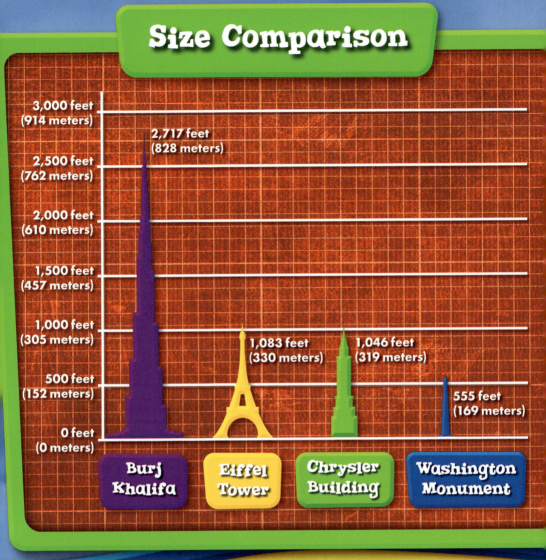

The tower has three **observation decks**. The highest is at 906 feet (276 meters).

The Eiffel Tower Today

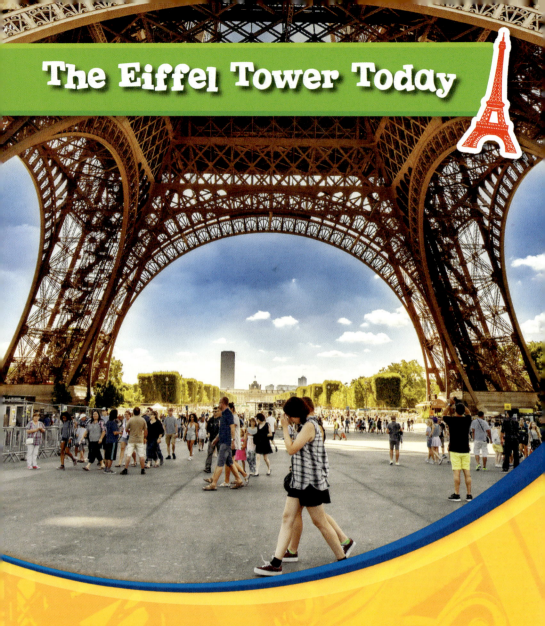

Nearly 7 million tourists visit the Eiffel Tower each year. It is one of France's most popular tourist spots.

The tower is painted about every seven years. This protects the iron.

The Eiffel Tower got **wind turbines** in 2015. A rain water collection system was also added. These make the tower more Earth-friendly.

The Eiffel Tower has changed a lot over time. More changes are likely to come!

Glossary

antennas—rods, wires, or other devices used to send and receive radio or TV signals

architect—a person who designs and plans buildings

concrete—relating to a hard, strong building material made with cement, sand, rocks, and water

design—to make a plan for a building, object, or pattern

engineer—a person with science training who designs and builds machines, systems, or structures

girders—large support beams in buildings and bridges

lattice—relating to a structure or framework made of crossed metal or wood strips

monument—a building or other structure built to honor someone or something

observation decks—platforms built so that people can look out at a view

rivets—short metal bolts or pins used to hold two pieces of metal together

telegraph—relating to a system for sending messages using electrical signals

tourists—people who travel to visit another place

wind turbines—large machines that change wind into electrical energy; energy is the power to make things work.

To Learn More

AT THE LIBRARY

Colson, Rob. *The Spectacular Science of Buildings: From Ancient Wonders to Modern Megastructures.* London, U.K.: Kingfisher, 2023.

Rossiter, Brienna. *Eiffel Tower.* Mendota Heights, Minn.: Apex Editions, 2024.

Smith, Emma Bland. *How Science Saved the Eiffel Tower.* North Mankato, Minn.: Capstone, 2022.

ON THE WEB

FACTSURFER

Factsurfer.com gives you a safe, fun way to find more information.

1. Go to www.factsurfer.com.

2. Enter "Eiffel Tower" into the search box and click 🔍.

3. Select your book cover to see a list of related content.

Index

1889 World's Fair, 8
antennas, 16
arches, 10, 11
architect, 10
base, 10
builders, 13
building location, 5
building supplies, 13
concrete, 10
design, 8, 9
Eiffel, Gustave, 9, 14
engineer, 9
girders, 10, 11
history, 5, 8, 9, 10, 12, 13, 14, 16, 20
iron, 9, 12, 19
Le Jules Verne, 15
leaders, 8, 14
legs, 10
lights, 7
monument, 4, 8
observation decks, 16, 17

painted, 19
Paris, France, 4, 5
restaurants, 14, 15
rivets, 13
Sauvestre, Stephen, 10
science lab, 14
Seine River, 4
shops, 14
size, 5, 16, 17
telegraph station, 14
tourists, 6, 14, 18
views, 6
water collection system, 20
wind turbines, 20

The images in this book are reproduced through the courtesy of: Bulat.Iskhakov, front cover; Thomas Dutour, front cover (inset), background (throughout); dumpstock, front cover (inset); Katya Maush, icon (throughout); Pascale Gueret, p. 3; Adisa, p. 4; Brastock, p. 6; Mistervlad, p. 7; Universitäts-und Landesbibliothek Darmstadt/ Wikimedia, p. 8; Smith Archive/ Alamy Stock Photo, p. 9; Pierre Petit/ Wikimedia, p. 10; The History Collection/ Alamy Stock Photo, pp. 10-11; IanDagnall Computing/ Alamy Stock Photo, p. 12; wsfurlan, p. 13 (iron); Juhku, p. 13 (concrete); dimm3d, p. 13 (rivets); larisa_stock, p. 13 (paint); Photobeps, p. 13; Alexandra Lande, p. 14; Tom Craig/ Alamy Stock Photo, p. 15; ColorMaker, pp. 14-15; Massimo Parisi, pp. 16-17; Feel good studio, p. 18; Mistervlad, p. 19; moofushi, p. 20; saiko3p, pp. 20-21; Delphotostock, p. 23.